The Ancient Celtic Festivals
and How We Celebrate Them Today

The Ancient Celtic Festivals

and How We Celebrate Them Today

Clare Walker Leslie
Frank E. Gerace
Illustrations by Clare Walker Leslie

Inner Traditions
Rochester, Vermont

Inner Traditions International
One Park Street
Rochester, Vermont 05767
www.InnerTraditions.com

Library of Congress Cataloging-in-Publication Data

Leslie, Clare Walker.
    The ancient Celtic festivals and how we celebrate them today / Clare Walker
  Leslie and Frank Gerace.
      p. cm.
    Inlcudes bibliographical references and index.
    ISBN 0-89281-822-0 (alk. paper)
    1. Celts—Folklore. 2. Festivals—Juvenile literature. 3. Holidays—Juvenile literature. [1. Celts—Folklore. 2. Festivals. 3. Holidays.] I. Gerace, Frank. II. Title.

  GR137 .L47 2000
  398.26′089′916—dc21
                                                              00-039590

Printed and bound in Hong Kong

10 9 8 7 6 5 4 3 2 1

Text design and layout by Priscilla H. Baker
This book was typeset in stone serif

Authors' Note

As educators, it has been our concern to be as accurate and as clear in our descriptions as possible. As so little was written down about the ancient Celts during the time in which they lived, our research has been both extensive and fascinating. We have tried to depict the Celts as they once were, rather than through the interpretation of nineteenth- and twentieth-century literature. We take all responsibility for any errors or assumptions that may seem incorrect. And we thank our editor at Inner Traditions International, Laura Schlivek, for supporting this project.

Our fathers, they have said these things . . .
It's the land it is our wisdom
It's the land it shines us through
It's the land it feeds our children
It's the land
You cannot own the land
The land owns you.

—Lyrics from "Solid Ground"
by Dougie MacLean,
published by Limetree Arts and Music, Scotland

Contents

Where do these celebrations come from?

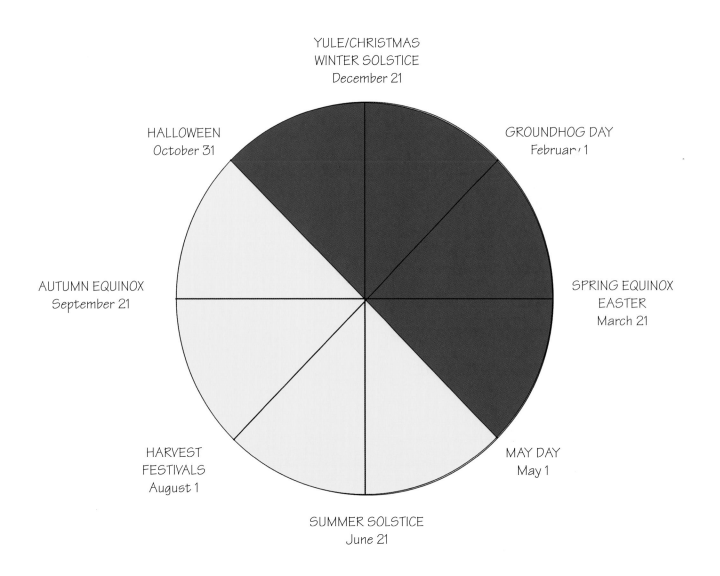

YULE/CHRISTMAS
WINTER SOLSTICE
December 21

GROUNDHOG DAY
February 1

HALLOWEEN
October 31

SPRING EQUINOX
EASTER
March 21

AUTUMN EQUINOX
September 21

MAY DAY
May 1

HARVEST
FESTIVALS
August 1

SUMMER SOLSTICE
June 21

Introduction

Have you ever wondered why we celebrate Halloween on October 31 rather than on some other date? Doesn't it seem strange that Groundhog Day falls on February 2, to celebrate spring, when groundhogs are still in the middle of winter's hibernation? Why is Christmas celebrated on December 25; why is Easter called Easter? None of this can be explained by our modern calendar, but it makes perfect sense when we look at the natural cycle of the seasons and the seasonal celebrations of older cultures.

Many of our modern holidays come from very ancient calendars that people brought to North America from their homelands in northern Europe and the British Isles. Though our style of celebration has changed over the centuries, these ancient festivals are reminders of how our northern European ancestors (like our ancestors from all over the world) once lived by the rising and setting of the moon, sun, stars, and planets.

Long before the time of Julius Caesar (and during his time as well) there were large groups of wandering people north of Rome, who measured time by their own calendar. Unlike the Roman calendar, which only measured the sun's passage across the sky, their calendar paid attention to the waxing and waning of the moon and to the positions of the stars as well. Because they were a farming civilization, the changing of the seasons was important to them, too, and their celebrations marked things like the birth of lambs and the harvesting of grain.

Who were these people? And how did their seasonal festivals change to become the holidays we celebrate today? To the Romans they were called the Galli or Gauls, to the Greeks they were the *keltoi*—

the "hidden people"—as they had no written language, their stories were "hidden" from other cultures.

They kept their traditions alive for centuries by telling stories and reciting poetry out loud. It would be impossible to write their stories down and still have them contain all the levels of meaning that a live storyteller could bring to them. It is from these stories, from artifacts found in ancient gravesites, and from accounts by Greek and Roman writers that we have learned about these fascinating but little-known people. Today, these northern European people are known collectively as the Celts (pronounced kelts). We think that the word *kilt* comes from the same Greek root, meaning "to hide" or "to conceal." Variations on their language can still be heard today in Gaelic (Scottish or Irish), Manx (on the Isle of Man), Welsh (in Wales), Cornish (in Cornwall, England), and Breton (in Brittany, France).

Among the many things the Celts have left us is their yearly seasonal calendar. In modern times, with our electric lights and store-bought foods, our survival no longer depends on understanding seasonal changes. But we still need to honor the ways of the earth, as our ancestors did all over the world. And so, we dedicate this book to the Celts themselves, and to all our ancestors, who lived by the rhythms of nature.

1

Since the creation of life on our planet, all living creatures have been affected by the Earth's spinning passage around the sun. The sun gives us our hours of light and dark, our days of rain and drought, our weeks of heat and cold, our seasons of growth and rest.

Early Calendars

Long, long ago, before there were clocks, radios, calendars or computers, our ancestors knew how to recognize the passage of the times of day, the shifts from drought to flood, and the seasons of growth and rest in the land around them. They needed to know these basic patterns of life to survive.

Those of us who live in a part of the world that has a climate like that of France, Germany, Austria, northern Spain, England, Scotland, or Wales—the countries where the Celts lived from around 700 B.C. to the first century A.D.—know that spring comes between February and May, summer comes between May and June, autumn comes between August and September, and winter can begin by October 31.

If you live in a warmer climate, like Texas, Florida, Australia, Brazil, or Mexico, your calendar will follow different seasonal rhythms.

The word *season* comes from the old French word *seson* meaning: "a period in which a special type of agricultural work is done and a particular type of weather prevails."*

Imagine what the world was like in 700 B.C. There was no electricity, so the only sources of light were the sun, moon, and stars and the man-made fires, which also provided heat when the sun did not. When the sun went down, it was very dark and, in winter, very cold.

Seasonal changes were what the Celts, and all early peoples, watched to determine times for travel, planting, festivals, harvest, breeding, rest, and activity—the basic calendar for their year.

Webster's New Collegiate Dictionary.

If you were a sixth-century Celt, with no chance of electricity, imagine what 5:00 P.M. in winter would look like—both outdoors and indoors—DARK.

The Celts' survival depended on the seasons of planting and harvest and the life cycles of their animal stock. They based their year on:

- end of winter/beginning of spring, when calves and lambs are born, and birds begin to reappear

- beginning of summer, when cattle and sheep are taken to upper pastures, gardens are planted, men and women marry, when men leave for battle and women follow cattle to the high meadows

- end of summer/beginning of fall, when gardens are harvested, birds begin migrating, and cattle and sheep return for slaughter or winter stay

- end of fall/beginning of winter, when the harvest is in, the winter home prepared, and the agricultural year ends

Great feasts, parties, family and tribal gatherings, and occasions for political decision-making marked each of these seasonal changes.

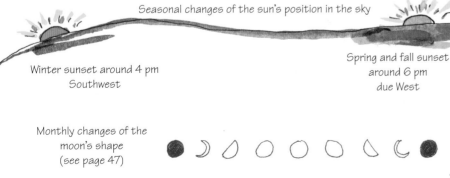

Seasonal changes of the sun's position in the sky

Winter sunset around 4 pm
Southwest

Spring and fall sunset around 6 pm
due West

You can observe the sun's changing positions yourself by noticing direction of daily shadows and where sun sets—and rises—month after month. It shifts through the seasons giving more and less light (see pages 27, 48, 50).

Summer sunset around 9 pm
Northwest

Hourly shifts of particular constellations, planets, and star patterns throughout the night sky (see page 49)

Monthly changes of the moon's shape (see page 47)

3

Part I
Who Were the Celts?

The Celts were a collection of tribal peoples who appeared in Europe around the seventh or eighth century B.C., possibly from as far away as Turkey or India. Although they lived in separate tribes, similarities in their arts, physical makeup, social structure, and most importantly, in their languages, allow us today to consider them as a single people. The artifacts that they buried with their dead also give us clues to their Celtic identity. It is important to remember that when we speak of the Celts we are speaking of many different tribes. Despite their similarities, there were many differences between the tribes, which is one reason they never united as a single Celtic nation.

They spread, by both peaceful and warlike means, over a large part of Europe. Their skill in metalwork, raising animals, and preserving food with salt helped them create a successful culture. While the Celts were farmers and herdspeople, they were also fierce hunters and warriors, known to paint blue designs on their skin, using a vegetable dye called woad, before going into battle. In those days every culture had to be a fighting culture in order to survive. The women could be as fierce as the men. Indeed, the great Irish hero Cuchulainn learned his legendary battle skills from a woman. The Celts had iron swords and used horses in battle, which gave them a big advantage over the people they conquered. In fact, one of the main reasons the Romans developed the military skill and strength we know them for today was to fend off the Celtic military threat.

The Romans fought Celtic people in the Gallic Wars. Caesar wrote much of what is known about the Celts but we must read what he wrote carefully. Imagine what it would be like if your history were written down only by your enemies. It would probably be a pretty biased view. So we have to remember that the popular Greek and Roman image of the Celts as "barbarians" was a prejudiced picture.

One fascinating aspect of the Celts is their mythology. As the Celts chose not to have a written language, much of their own view of their history was woven into their mythological tales, which they memorized and recited out loud until the ninth century A.D. Many of these stories that survive today were written down in the Middle Ages by Christian monks who heard the tales from storytellers. But the Celtic mythology was full of magic, so the monks changed the stories to make them fit with the teachings of the Christian Church. Once again, the Celtic point of view has been altered. As with *any* history, what we read about the Celts has to be very carefully sorted out between fact and fiction.

The Celts often wove wool with plaids and stripes which may be the early origin of kilts. They loved jewelry and would paint their bodies with a blue dye—woad—before battle.

Women held high positions in a tribe

Often clean-shaven, with long mustaches

Limed, pointy hair to make them look scary for warfare

Distinctive neck torc

To the Greeks and Romans the Celts were tall, blond, and ruddy complexioned

Where the Celts Lived

When we talk about the Celts, we are actually talking about people from many different countries over a very long period of time. From about 700 B.C. to A.D. 600 Celtic civilizations existed across the face of Europe, including, of course, the British Isles. While these various groups had a lot in common, they had many differences as well. By breaking them into smaller groups we can discuss them a little more accurately.

The heartland of the ancient Celts was the land called Gaul—today this region consists of northern Italy, Switzerland, France, and Belgium. The Gauls were a powerful threat to their southern neighbors, in terms of both culture and military might. They sacked Rome in 390 B.C. and Delphi in 279 B.C.

In this book, we will look most closely at the British Celts, who include the Irish, Scots, and Welsh, as their descendants were among the first Europeans to settle in America, bringing their traditions and festivals with them. The Irish and the Highland Scots are important to us as they have kept alive much of the Celtic culture that flourished in Britain before Rome invaded in A.D. 43. The Irish were never conquered by the Romans, though there are remains of Roman forts on the Irish coast. The Highlands of Scotland were isolated areas, well north of Hadrian's Wall (which separated Roman Britain from Celtic lands to the north), so Roman influence there was nowhere near what it was in conquered areas, like England. The Bretons in Brittany (part of France) are very close in spirit and culture to the Welsh, having common tribal ancestors.

The earliest known Celtic site was discovered in a lakebed in Hallstadt, Austria, a small village in the Alps. This salt-mining community was discovered in 1846 and has been dated to around 700 B.C. The salt preserved the artifacts found there. Another village that existed later, around 500 B.C., has been excavated in LaTene, Switzerland. There were also Celtic civilizations in what is now modern Turkey, where the Celts were called Galatians, and in the north of Spain in the province called Galicia today.

Over the coming centuries the Celts were gradually defeated throughout much of Europe. This is because they never united as a nation with a unified military force, the way the Greeks and Romans did. By the first century B.C. they were found mainly in the westernmost parts of Europe. But even though their armies were defeated, Celtic culture was never entirely destroyed. Though they merged with Roman culture, many of the old customs lived on, especially out in the countryside.

The Celts became known for producing certain items. Between about 700 BC–200 AD various Celtic tribes, in different regions of their civilization, were powerful in trade as well as in military power.

TRADE ITEMS:

Woven cloth from wool and flax and animal hides

Gold

Tin, lead, iron, copper, bronze, silver products. Celts used iron in wheels and in ploughs and for weapons

Mined salt

Grains for bread, porridge, beer (the Celts were very fond of Roman wine and the Romans were very fond of Celtic beer)

Jewelry

Map

The CELTIC WORLD by around 250 BC

Earliest evidence of Celts in Europe:
La Tene = 700 BC
Hallstadt = 500 BC

Indo-European origins of the Celtic peoples from somewhere north and east of the Black Sea, perhaps as far as India

Tara
London
Leiden
Laon
BRITANY
Alesia
(Switzerland)
La Tene
Hallstadte
(Austria)
GALLIA (Gaul)
GALICIA (Spain)
GALLIA CISALPINA
ROME (Italy)
GREECE
Delphi
Black Sea
Galatia (Asia Minor)

North Africa was along the trade routes of the seafaring Celts

5

The Druids

The druids were very important in Celtic society. They were the priests, priestesses, and educated leaders; the lawyers and judges of the Celtic people, as well as the teachers of the nobles. All their teachings were spoken in long poems rather than written down; some were even sung. The druid poets had great power. Their words were feared by all, as a bard's satire could cause a king to lose his kingdom. The Celtic people believed that the druids had magical powers and could see into the future.

The druids kept alive the family histories of the tribes and leaders. They ruled on cases involving broken laws and advised the kings and queens of the Celtic world on all matters. When important decisions had to be made, they were traditionally the first to speak. Their word was respected beyond the word of any local tribal government.

The Romans outlawed the druidic order because of their power and influence. When the Romans attacked the druid sanctuary at Anglesea, the Roman legions were so terrified of the black-robed druidesses on the opposite shore that their leaders had to force them into battle at swordpoint. In general, the Romans were very tolerant of religious differences and did not punish people for holding different views as long as they paid lip service to the divinity of the Caesar. The Christians and the druids were the only religious groups they outlawed because both threatened Rome's political power.

Ceremonial trumpet

Druid priests were both men and women who officiated over many tribal events, such as blessing crops and giving offerings to Lugh, Lord of the Sun, one of their many gods.
According to accounts by the Romans, druids wore white as well as dark-colored robes.

6

The word *druid* has many possible roots. It could come from words meaning "wise," "hard," or "oak." As the Celts' language contained so many layers of meaning that a phrase could mean many things at once, it seems somehow appropriate that all these different words relate to the word *druid*.

The druids were responsible for setting the laws for all the Celtic tribes. Among other things, these laws set the times when festivals would be celebrated. All the druids were trained in Ireland, so there was an underlying common teaching to the beliefs of all the Celts, despite their differing local customs.

The Celts and Nature

The Celts, along with most ancient peoples, had a great respect for nature. The effects of the natural world determined whether they lived or died. If the weather was bad and the growing season suffered, they risked starvation. Natural disasters could make wild animals become dangerous enemies as well because the animals' own starvation made them desperate enough to risk attacking humans. If the winter was exceptionally cold, the Celts risked freezing to death unless they had shelter that was safe and warm. For heat, they needed firewood, which came from the huge forests all around. So their relationship with nature was a part of their everyday life.

More urban cultures like Greece and Rome organized their societies around city-states. Because they were country people, the Celtic civilizations organized theirs around the land. Their relationship to the land was very important. Changes in the land and weather were watched very carefully and interpreted for the kings by druids. Their traditions preserved the knowledge of how to live on the land through the changes of time, season, and weather. For this reason, even though they were defeated by the Roman army and eventually converted to Christianity, these peoples of the northern

Dwellings were made of rushes, wood, stone, and some form of mud

Celtic dwellings in Britain, Spain, and Portugal were usually round, while in other areas of Europe they were square or oblong

forests kept alive many of their customs, their land-based religion, and their unwritten seasonal calendars, even to the present day.

Water was very important to all the ancient people. The Romans were the first to make aqueducts to carry water from one place to another. Before that, farmers had to use different ways to irrigate their crops. Drinking water had to come from clean rivers, springs, and wells. And indeed, rivers, springs, and wells are featured in many traditional Celtic stories. As these places were so important to the Celts' survival, they were considered sacred. The stories tell of gods

and goddesses who became rivers or springs and of the guardians who protected them. Many rivers in Celtic countries are named after these same gods and goddesses. Special healing was available at many of the springs and wells. People with health problems would go bathe in the spring or drink water from the well. Then they tied colored ribbons on nearby trees as thanks for the healing they received.

Because they worked with the forces of nature, the druids never built temples or churches. It was perfectly appropriate for them to hold their religious services in the open, natural world. They performed their rituals in sacred groves—special groups of trees that held deep meaning for their tribes. As all life was sacred to them, they did not make statues of their gods and goddesses. If the goddess was embodied by the river, there was no need to make a statue of her that looked like a human. This nature-based view was very different from the way the Greeks and Romans looked at their gods and goddesses.

But one thing the Celts did have in common with the Greeks and Romans was that all three cultures were fond of telling stories about their gods, goddesses, heroes, and heroines. Many of the stories from the Irish *Book of Invasions,* for example, are about the Tuatha De Danaan (the Children of Dana). These are stories of great battles, fought by mighty heroes. The Tuatha De Danaan are actually ancient Celtic gods and goddesses. Celtic tales also include many great heroes, like Cuchulainn, who is like an Irish Hercules.

Animals always played a great part in Celtic life. The Celts raised animals like oxen to use for labor and sheep, goats, and pigs for food and wool or hides. They used horses for battle. In their stories, great adventures are centered around cattle raids, herds of swine, and hunts for mysterious white stags. Another common theme in adventure stories was one kingdom's stealing of rare animals from another kingdom.

Many of the gods and goddesses were known by the animals they were associated with, like Cerridwen, the Welsh goddess who is associated with a white sow, or Rhiannon, another Welsh goddess who is associated with a white horse. These special animals are called "totem animals." The god Bran (or Vran) was a great hero and adventurer. His name means "raven." When he was killed in battle, his head continued to live and talk. He asked his men to bury his head on the White Mount in what is now London. Here he would guard and protect England until his head was dug up. Legend has it that King Arthur dug Bran's head up because he wanted to be the only hero responsible for England's welfare. Nowadays, there are actual ravens in the Tower of London and it is said that when the ravens leave the tower, England will fall.

Many heroes are associated with an animal that was born at the same time they were. Sometimes the human and the animal are raised together. Sometimes the association with a totem animal comes later, at an important event in the hero's life. The name of the great hero Cuchulainn means "hound of Culann." His name at birth was Setanta. He got the name Cuchulainn by fighting and killing the guard dog of the chief he served, then offering to become the guard dog himself, until a new one could be found. From that point on, eating dog meat was forbidden to him. In Celtic tradition, heroes are usually given a series of things they must never do. These prohibitions are called *geasas*.

The tradition of human association with a special totem animal carried on through the Dark Ages, when the early Celtic Christian Church was at its strongest. Many of the Saints, who helped spread the Church throughout England, Ireland, and Scotland were associated with birds, otters, dogs, and horses and are still shown with these animals in pictures today. Saint Kevin is always pictured with blackbirds, Saint Maedoc is associated with the stag, and Saint Kentigern with a salmon.

The alphabet the druids used was also tied to nature. Although the druids did not write anything down, there are carvings on stones in northern Europe that use a special alphabet called *ogham*. They appear to have been carved from around A.D. 300 on. The alphabet is different from our ABCs. The names of the letters refer to the Irish names of plants or animals. For example, in tree ogham the letters represented the names of trees. In bird ogham the Celts used the same order of letters (which started B, L, N, F, S, not A, B, C, D, E!) but instead of representing the names of trees, the letters represented the names of birds. We know about this alphabet from the later writings of bards and storytellers who *did* write things down. There are many types of ogham mentioned in their poems and stories and most of them refer to things in the natural world.

Much of what we know of the later Celtic cultures comes from Irish texts and some Welsh texts, all written down much later, but containing within them elements of the original storytelling traditions of the Celtic past. When we look at French and British Celtic culture, we divide it into the time before the Romans invaded, the time when the Romans ruled, and the time after they were driven out. The Romans had a very strong influence on all the countries they had contact with. Later the Angles, the Saxons, and the Jutes invaded Britain, as did the Vikings, all leaving their influences on the culture. And, just as with any culture today, some Celtic societies were rich and some were poor. So, you see, it can be misleading to make generalized statements about *all* the Celts at once. But we can safely say that all the Celts had a close relationship with nature.

The Celts evolved markings for inscriptions on stones, primarily for honoring the dead, a place, or an event. This stone uses an Ogham alphabet.

Bronze boar from Hungary, 2nd century B.C.

Celtic gold and iron coins found in many tombs

Design embossed on pot from Essex, England Iron Age

A way of learning about the early Celts is from objects found in burial sites throughout Europe

Pre Celtic

The Megalithic Age

The great stone monuments like Stonehenge and Avebury are built (4000–3000 B.C.)
The Pyramids of Egypt are built (2800 B.C.)

Standing stones

The Bronze Age (2000 B.C.)

The Iron Age (800 B.C.)

Height of Celtic Expansion/Civilization

Hallstadt civilization—earliest archeological evidence of a Celtic people living in Hallstadt, Austria, around 700 B.C.
LaTene civilization—Celtic burial site in LaTene, Switzerland, around 500 B.C.
Celtic tribes cross the Alps and attack Rome (400 B.C.)
Celts sack Rome (390 B.C.)
Celtic Galatians sack the Temple of Apollo at Delphi in Greece (279 B.C.)
Celts defeated by the Greeks at Pergamon in Turkey (230 B.C.)
Hannibal and his army, half of whom are Celts, cross the Alps (218 B.C.)
Rome attacks and conquers Southern Gaul (125 B.C.)
Julius Caesar invades Celtic Gaul (58 B.C.)
Vercingetorix, the Gaullish chief, attacks Julius Caesar, but ultimately loses in Alesia, France (52–45 B.C.)

Curving, floral style of La Tene helped define Celtic Art

Metal objects found in early grave sites

Statue of Vercingetorix in France

Claudius orders the invasion of Britain (A.D. 43)
Boudicca, Queen of a Celtic tribe called the Iceni, living in southern England, leads a rebellion against the Roman invaders of Britain (A.D. 60)
Rome attacks and conquers England (A.D. 62)
Hadrian's Wall is built, separating Roman Britain from the Picts and Celts to the north (A.D. 122)

Decline of Celtic Influence

The Dark Ages

The Romans leave Britain as Angles, Saxons, and Jutes invade (A.D. 367)
The Roman Empire falls and Constantine and Constantinople in Asia Minor rise to power (A.D. 330–460)
Saint Patrick arrives in Ireland to convert the pagan Celts to the new Roman religion (A.D. 432)
The reign of Arthur (A.D. 450–525), a Celtic warlord who briefly united the tribes against Saxon invaders
Saint Augustine converts much of Britain to Christianity (A.D. 597)
The Book of Kells, an eighth-century manuscript from the monastery of Kells in Ireland, fully decorated with Celtic art (A.D. 800)

Statue of Boudicca in London

Celtic Christian Monk AD 550

King Arthur

The Middle Ages

Celtic Culture goes under-ground

Macbeth, the last elected Celtic King of Scotland (A.D. 1040)
The Norman conquest of Britain (A.D. 1066)
Geoffrey of Monmouth "transcribes" *Vita Merlini* and *The History of the Kings of England* (A.D. 1120)
Celtic culture outlawed in England (A.D. 1500)
Celtic Scotland defeated by England at the Battle of Culloden Moor, Celtic culture outlawed in Scotland (A.D. 1745)

Book of Kells

Macbeth

Battle of Culloden Moor

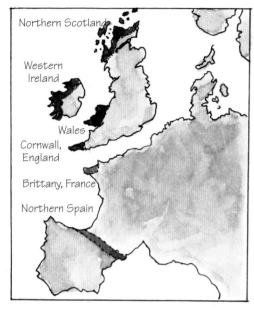

In Northern Europe

In North America

 Areas where old customs still cling, and, in some areas, are being revived today

 Areas where traces of Celtic culture can be found

The Celts Today

Old Celtic societies thrived in remote parts of Britain through the seventeenth century, until the battle between Gaelic people and the Anglo-Normans became a battle between Catholicism and Protestantism. Gaelic Scotland was defeated by the English at the bloody Battle of Culloden Moor in 1745, whereupon Bonnie Prince Charlie, bagpipes, and kilts were outlawed. It became a crime, punishable by death, to sing the old songs, or to play the harp or the bagpipes. The English were intent on wiping out all traces of Celtic culture, which they viewed as a political threat.

The destructive Highland Clearances forced many Gaelic Scots off the land and sent them to the new world of North America as indentured servants—virtual slaves who had to work for no pay for years to buy their freedom. Many were sent to the mountains of Appalachia and to the Virginia coloniesin the United States. Others were settled in Nova Scotia (whose name means New Scotland), Canada. Today the old culture and the spoken Gaelic language remain only in the western Highlands and islands off the coast of Scotland, much as Native American culture has been confined to reservations and limited areas in the United States.

In Ireland, the potato famine of the 1840s and the religious and ethnic wars that followed destroyed much of Ireland's Gaelic-speaking population, leaving only isolated Gaelic-speaking communities on the outer western edges of the Irish coastline and in a few other remote areas. Many Irish, in migrating to America and other parts of the world, brought their old ways with them. Others, as is common for victims of political repression, were embarrassed by their own history and tried to hide their roots. Even so, much of their culture has managed to survive into modern times.

Many of the European countries we know today were constantly invaded over the last 3,000 years. Their borders have changed many times, and the people who live there have the blood of many different cultures mixed together in their veins. The major wars that we study, and the minor ones that we don't know about, have all had their effects. As we look back, we can see that these people of the British Isles and northern Europe have, in time, become a blend of Celtic, Roman, Anglo-Saxon, Viking, and numerous other tribal intermarriages. But the spirit that was Celtic has remained in many of their customs, traditions, music, art, stories, and holidays. *The seasonal calendar of the Celts, begun in a mysterious past and never written down, is still with us today.*

Part II
The Ancient Celtic Festivals

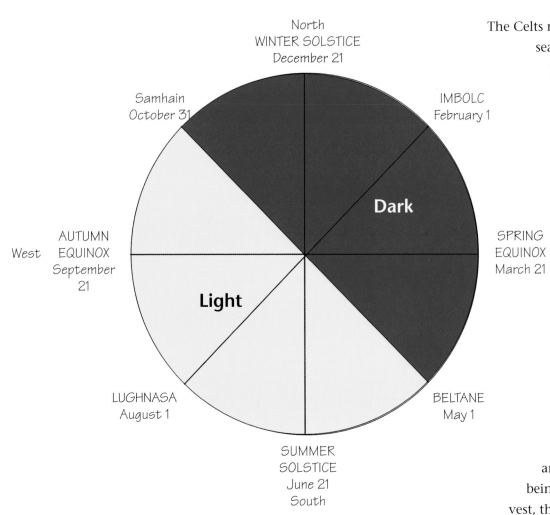

North
WINTER SOLSTICE
December 21

Samhain
October 31

IMBOLC
February 1

AUTUMN
EQUINOX
September
21

West

Dark

SPRING
EQUINOX
March 21

East

Light

LUGHNASA
August 1

BELTANE
May 1

SUMMER
SOLSTICE
June 21
South

The Celts marked their year not by political or religious dates, but by seasonal changes. In order to explain the divisions of their year in modern terms, we have represented the year as a circle here to show where the Celtic festivals fall on our present-day calendar. *We have no evidence that the Celts ever used a circular calendar themselves.*

• The word *calendar* is from the Latin *kalendae*, which was the first day of the month when the *kalends* or debts were to be paid in the Roman world.

• Today, the Chinese, Jewish, Muslim, and Hindu calendars still follow the moon's daily phase changes, adjusting to keep up with the modern solar calendar ($29\frac{1}{2}$ days for each complete cycle). Their New Year's Day is not on January 1, but on movable days at other points of the year.

• To the Celts, dates were never fixed, nor were months absolute. The calendar's turning was determined by events of nature: the light being bright and the ground being warm enough to plant, the sun being at the right position, the crops being ready to harvest, the cattle coming back from pasture, the lambs being born, the moon being full, and so forth.

Whether we are aware of it or not, *in North America,* we still honor aspects of the ancient Celtic calendar.

Ancient Calendar	Gaelic* word	Modern calendar
1. When calves, lambs, and human babies are born.	Imbolc or Oimelc	Groundhog Day Candlemas February 2
2. When sheep and cattle are taken to upper pastures, gardens are planted, young men and women marry, men go to battle, women tend the gardens and livestock.	Beltane	May Day May 1
3. When fields and gardens are harvested, and cattle and sheep return from the hills.	Lughnasa	August Harvest Days August 1–15
4. The harvest is in, grains are prepared for storage, animals are slaughtered and food and homes are prepared for the coming winter months. The agricultural year ends.	Samhain	Halloween All Saint's Day October 31– November 2

IMBOLC
Spring

BELTANE
Summer

Although the Wheel of the Year is not really an ancient Celtic calendar, it can be a useful tool for showing how the Celts and other ancient peoples most likely viewed the year in a nonlinear fashion. The seasonal festivals and the circular progression of the year work very well with what we currently know of Celtic cultures. There are other circular calendars that we can trace back to ancient times. The Buddhists have one of the oldest on record with much of the same type of information.

Fragments of a bronze calendar that *is* Celtic have been found in Coligny, France. While the calendar is not circular, it combines the elements of a solar calendar with a lunar calendar. There are only pieces of it left, as it was apparently broken and then buried, perhaps as an offering. It shows that both the solar year and the lunar month were used in the Celts' reckoning of time. This calendar, called the Coligny calendar (see page 15), was found in 1897 and is believed to have been made during the first century A.D.

LUGHNASA
Autumn

---

*Gaelic—A branch of the Celtic languages including Irish Gaelic, Scottish Gaelic, and Manx (Isle of Man, off the coast of England), as defined by *Webster's New Collegiate Dictionary*. The Gaelic names for the festival days can be translated to: *Imbolc*—"in the womb," *Oimelc*—"ewe's milk," *Beltane*—"fires of Bel," *Lughnasa*—"festival of Lugh," *Samhain*— "summer's end."

SAMHAIN
Winter

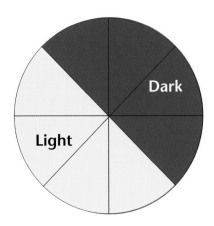

Even though the Celts probably never drew out a round calendar for a wall chart, by using a circle we are trying to present a way of understanding time and calendars that is more like the way the Celts would have understood the year. We are not trying to apply our current ideas of time to their world. We use a calendar with fixed dates for celebrations (as this has evolved to suit the needs of our times), whereas the Celts, who had no written language, used observable events to mark the passage of time. They used the sun, moon, and stars, as well as the weather and changes in the land around them, as indicators of when certain tasks were to be done and festivals celebrated. Your understanding of time will change and grow as you learn to tell time by watching the natural changes in the world around you.

The Celts divided the year into two parts, dark and light, winter and summer. (If you live in northern Europe, or in the northern part of North America, you know that the darker months fall between November 1 and May 1 and the lighter months fall between May 1 and November 1.) For the Celts, everything began in darkness. So each new day began at sundown and the new year began at sundown on Samhain (pronounced sow-wen, from the Gaelic, "summer's end"), beginning the dark half of the year. This holiday is celebrated today as Halloween or All Hallows' Eve, from sunset on October 31 until sunset on November 1. The day that marked the end of the dark half of the year was Beltane (pronounced bel-tayne), named after Bel, a Celtic sun god, celebrated today from the evening of April 30 through May 1. These days marked the changes from winter to summer in Celtic traditions.

The Pleiades, or "seven sisters" (a star cluster of seven or more stars in the constellation Taurus, 400 light years away), was very important to many ancient cultures, including the Celts. They would watch for its position in the sky and use that as a way to mark time.

In late October the Pleiades can be seen rising in the eastern sky, one hour after sunset.

The Pleiades reaches its highest point around midnight on what we call October 31. During the six weeks between our present day April 15 to May 31 (approximately), the Pleiades is not visible at all in the latitudes of northern Europe. At some point in this six-week period, the constellation would be at its "lowest" point in the sky, or directly below where it was on October 31. Its placement at this low point would occur during what we would think of as the first week of May. So, at Samhain the Pleiades was at its highest point in the night sky and at Beltane it was at its lowest.

We know that some Celtic tribes celebrated Samhain on the first full moon after the Pleiades was at a peak, others on the new moon. Others, perhaps, celebrated on the first night the weather permitted. It was not unusual for people to calculate the time for celebrating a particular festival slightly differently. An example of variable calculation that we can see today is the way Eastern and Western Christian churches calculate the date for celebrating Easter. The Western Church celebrates Easter on the first Sunday after the first full moon after the spring equinox. The Eastern church celebrates it two weeks later. But the celebration of the day holds the same meaning for both groups.

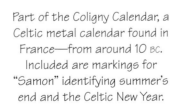

Part of the Coligny Calendar, a Celtic metal calendar found in France—from around 10 BC. Included are markings for "Samon" identifying summer's end and the Celtic New Year.

THE ANCIENT FESTIVALS

SAMHAIN
October 31
(beginning of the dark
half of the year)

IMBOLC
February 1
(halfway through
the dark time)

LUGHNASA
August 1
(halfway through
the light time)

BELTANE
May 1
(end of the dark
half of the year)

Now we cut the circle into quarters, so there are two periods of darkness and two of light. These midway points in the dark and light parts of the year are celebrated by Imbolc or Oimelc (pronounced im-olk) on February 1, and Lughnasa (pronounced loo-nas-ah) on August 1.

Imbolc, or Oimelc (meaning "ewe's milk" in Gaelic), was halfway between Samhain and Beltane. This festival marked the time when the ewes gave birth to their lambs. Halfway between Beltane and Samhain was Lughnasa. This was a festival of the god Lugh, another Celtic sun god. It marked the beginning of the harvest season, just after the first crops were harvested. Thus it was a time to celebrate. The actual timing of the festivals to celebrate these events seems to have been determined as much by the weather and changes in the land as by the signs in the sky. There would be no festival to celebrate the first harvest until the first harvest was brought in. Similarly, when the daylight hours began to noticeably lengthen and the weather got warmer, sheep would give birth to their lambs. Then the births would be celebrated.

As far as we can tell from surviving records, the solstices and equinoxes do not seem to have played a major role in British and Irish Celtic celebrations until after the Romans conquered Britain. Celebrations of the solstices and equinoxes probably came from Celtic contact with Germanic peoples, such as the Vikings, Angles, Saxons, and Jutes, who

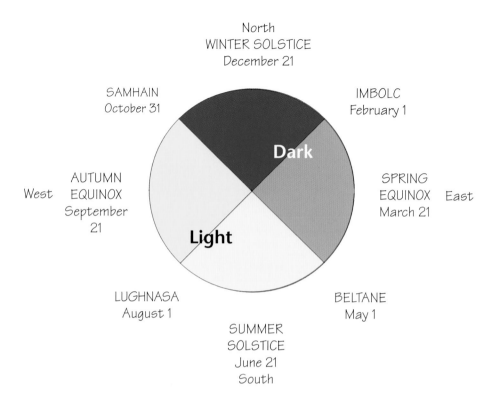

North
WINTER SOLSTICE
December 21

SAMHAIN
October 31

IMBOLC
February 1

Dark

AUTUMN
West   EQUINOX
September
21

SPRING
EQUINOX   East
March 21

Light

LUGHNASA
August 1

BELTANE
May 1

SUMMER
SOLSTICE
June 21
South

This calendar followed the agricultural divisions of the year for the Celts. But since religion and nature were intertwined for them, these were occasions for sacred and mystical celebrations as well. It is important to keep in mind that the four agricultural divisions were celebrated around the dates of October 31, February 1, May 1, and August 1. But the actual dates of the celebrations varied from year to year according to celestial variations, the weather, and how busy people were. Also, the festivals would last for several days. Clans gathered, families reunited, and many people traveled long distances to attend the festivities. When Christianity came along, it made sense to combine the old Celtic celebrations with the new Christian ones. Can you see where Christmas, Easter, and Halloween fit in?

invaded Britain during the Dark Ages after the Romans left. If you look at the circle to the left you will notice something interesting—the solstices and equinoxes cut each of the quarters we have defined exactly in half. Halfway between Samhain and Imbolc is the winter solstice (roughly six weeks from each). At the other end of that line, halfway between Beltane and Lughnasa, is the summer solstice. Adding the final line, we place the spring or vernal equinox halfway between Imbolc and Beltane and its counterpart, the autumn equinox, halfway between Lughnasa and Samhain (also roughly six weeks from each).

The key social events in the lives of these tribal Celts were the festivals that took place on each holiday. These festivals had religious, as well as social and agricultural, aspects. As life was a combination of all these different elements, it seems only fitting that the celebrations would include both social and spiritual activities. The fair at Lughnasa in Telltown, Ireland, for example, had great horse races. The fair was held in honor of Tailtiu, the foster mother of the God Lugh, and horses were sacred to her. The people who gathered for this great harvest festival celebrated the bounty of the land with the fruits of the first harvest and participated in games and contests. Attendance at these fairs was mandated by Irish law, which also defined strict codes of behavior. We know this from an old book of Irish laws.

Some of the oldest translated works we have are from Ireland and date to around A.D. 300. We have the stories in the Irish *Book of Invasions* that tell us how, mythologically, Ireland was settled by different groups of invaders. It tells the stories of the early races of gods and goddesses who came to Ireland. There are other old texts that tell us the stories behind the names of many places. There are ancient books of laws that tell us what was important to the Irish legally and how legal problems were resolved. When we read these old surviving records today we can see how the ancient Irish lived. There are many more books in university libraries that have not been translated yet. No doubt we could learn all sorts of new information from them, once they are translated from the ancient Irish.

The calendar we have used in this book is based on the changing seasons. We can see how each season was marked by a festival, and how each festival had a different spiritual meaning attached to it. We can also see the different social aspects of the festivals. So, our simple observational calendar tells us much more as we take a closer look at the lives of people who celebrated these festivals.

Depending on how far south or how far north you live, sunrise and sunset times vary. We have chosen London time for describing day length at the time of the ancient Samhain, Beltane, Imbolc, and Lughnasa Festivals. Modern London time corresponds pretty closely to the hours of daylight the northern European Celts would have had.

On Samhain cattle were driven between two fires to ritually cleanse them before the winter began.

Samhain—Around October 31

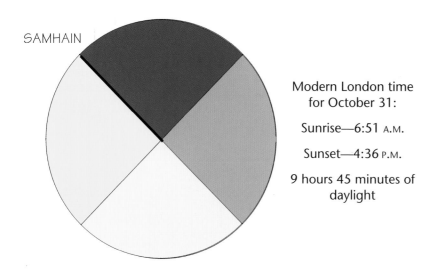

SAMHAIN

Modern London time for October 31:

Sunrise—6:51 A.M.

Sunset—4:36 P.M.

9 hours 45 minutes of daylight

Samhain is from an old Gaelic word meaning "summer's end" and for the northern European Celts it marked the end of the agricultural year and the beginning of a new year. It was a time when the killing frosts came, animals were brought in for the winter or slaughtered, and the last of the harvesting was complete. It was also a time for great feasting, merrymaking, and family gatherings, especially if the year had been a good one.

The Coligny Calendar referred to this festival as the "Three Nights of Summer's End." There was the last night of the old year, the first night of the new year and the night in between that belonged to no time. Samhain came at an important time in the Celtic year, as people made the transition from summer to winter. They prepared to spend the winter indoors, with stores of grain, dried meats and fruits, and winter vegetables for themselves, and with grains and hay for their animals. It was a time to decide which animals would be used for next year's breeding and to evaluate the health of the rest of the animals. Only the healthiest animals would be kept alive through the winter.

In addition, the warriors had returned from battle so men and women were together again. This was the time for prearranged marriages to begin in earnest as the long winter set in.

To mark these important transitions, ritual observances as well as legal assemblies were part of the festival celebrations. All household fires would be put out, then relit from a sacred bonfire (usually lit by a druid on a hilltop).* Cattle would be driven between two fires to symbolically cleanse them before the winter began. Tribal assemblies met to set rules and regulations for the tribe and pass judgments on the actions of the past year. In many areas, these would include a gathering of a great number of smaller tribes and chieftains. Many heroes in the old stories met their fated deaths at Samhain.

The Celts, who had a long history of ritually burying their dead with important possessions, were very aware of the presence of the dead and their ancestors. Samhain was a time when the veil between the worlds was thinnest—beings could cross from the world of the living to the world of the dead, and vice versa. The Celts did not fear their dead, but had feasts with them at this time of year to honor them. It was a time to show respect and hospitality to the spirits of their ancestors.

But not all the beings who crossed between the worlds were dead ancestors—this was also a night when the faery races could enter the human world, and many of them were mischief makers. People would leave out saucers of milk and sometimes even beer or whiskey for the faeries in hopes of being left alone. As people feared certain encounters with the faery races, they wore masks at Samhain to trick the faeries into not recognizing them. Any crops that were still unharvested at this point—the final harvest—were left in the fields for the faeries, and it was considered very bad luck to eat these leftovers. Many of our traditions of trick-or-treating and Mischief Night have roots in these early Celtic beliefs.

---

*As the sun and fire were critical elements to the survival of the Celts (and to all cultures for that matter), many rituals throughout the year involved fire and symbols of fire and the sun.

19

Beltane—Around May 1
The First Day of Summer

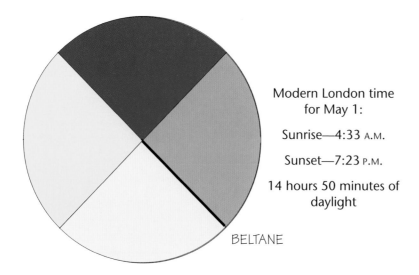

BELTANE

Modern London time
for May 1:

Sunrise—4:33 A.M.

Sunset—7:23 P.M.

14 hours 50 minutes of
daylight

Although Beltane was not the next holiday in the Celtic year, we want to talk about it next to remind you of how the Celtic year was divided into a dark half and a light half. While Samhain marked the beginning of the dark half of the year, Beltane comes exactly opposite it and marks the end of the dark time.

Beltane can be translated as "the fires of Bel." Bel seems to be connected with the old Celtic sun god Belenos, of Gaul. This is the time of year when winter has released its grip and the killing frosts are over. The light half of the year is beginning. Clans who have not seen each other all winter can get through the mud and rainy weather to celebrate winter's end.

The Pleiades' descent to the lowest point in the sky, where it was no longer visible, marked the start of Beltane. This second most important day was a great fire festival. In Ireland and the Highlands of Scotland, on the eve of the festival, all the household fires would be extinguished. As on Samhain, a sacred bonfire was lit on a hilltop, usually by a druid, and the house fires were all rekindled from that

fire as a symbol of life continuing. Beltane was the time to plant crops and the season for sending sheep and cattle out to pasture. This was also the battle season. The warriors were home from Samhain to Beltane, but they went off to battle from Beltane to Samhain.

While Samhain and Beltane were the key turning points of the Celtic year, each festival was given greater or lesser significance depending on where it was celebrated. So some Celtic tribes may have seen Samhain as their most important festival, while other Celtic tribes treated Beltane as the key celebration of the year and did all the important work of writing laws and passing tribal judgments at that time.

Agriculturally, the focus was on ploughing and planting the second round of crops. Early crops were usually hoed once in late April, and again in mid- to late May, to clear out weeds and thin the crop. In England, Wales, and southern Scotland, the maypole dance was more important as a Beltane observance than the ritual bonfire. The dancing was originally done around a tree that had all but its top branches cut off. The tree is a great symbol of the power of nature and of new life springing from the ground. The weaving of ribbons around the pole may have symbolized how daylight shortened in winter and lengthened in summer. And the finished pole, covered with intertwined streamers, celebrated the power of the earth. Today, the maypole has become a nonliving pole planted in the ground, usually in the center of a village or town. Morris dancers, wearing bells on their ankles and waving scarves, performed rhythmic dances to scare away the spirits of winter. Morris dances and mummers plays are full of ancient fertility symbols. In Cornwall today, morris dancing and maypoling are still very much a part of the annual Beltane festivities.

Moonrise, early evening

Druid priests relighting the Beltane fires

Animals blessed by a druid while going through a purifying fire

Animals head up to summer pastures

Blessing the plow

Planting of crops

Marriages, festivals, parties

Winter over, tribes and families reconnect

Couples connect

Men readying for battle

Field greens and flowers are collected for food and as dye plants

Imbolc—Around February 1
The First Day of Spring

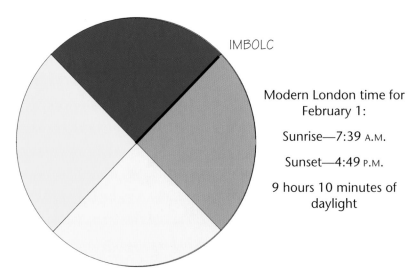

IMBOLC

Modern London time for February 1:

Sunrise—7:39 A.M.

Sunset—4:49 P.M.

9 hours 10 minutes of daylight

To understand why we look at Imbolc next, turn back to the circle on page 15. Notice how Imbolc comes halfway between Samhain and Beltane, exactly halfway through the dark side of the year.

Imbolc and Oimelc are two names from the Irish for a celebration held by our current reckoning on February 2, the halfway point of the dark half of the year. In the Scottish Highlands, the celebration was, and still is, held on February 13. *Imbolc* means "in the womb" and *Oimelc* means "ewe's milk" in old Gaelic. This was the time that the ewes gave birth, and the arrival of new lambs was the exciting event celebrated by this festival (this is still a time of celebration on farms where there are sheep). This birthing season marks an end to the dead season of winter as the sun gets higher in the sky and the days become noticeably longer. Remember that for the Celts this was not a fixed date.

Sheep have always been very important in Celtic lands, providing both food and clothing. The birth of lambs was cause for great rejoicing. Lambing, kidding, and calving mark the beginning of spring. Animals born in early spring will be ready to go to pasture by May or June. The Celts had to plan carefully to make sure their livestock would give birth at the right time. Cattle had to be bred the previous June.

The agricultural year began with ploughing the land to ready it for planting. Large stones were taken from the fields and used to build stone walls, remnants of which can still be seen today. As it was warmer earlier in northern Europe in the days of the early Celts, the planting season was longer. This allowed for crops to be harvested at three different times, as the crops planted later in the season usually ripened later in the year. Some of the main crops planted were wheat and barley and oats. Rye and millet were also grown.

As the main theme at this time of year was rebirth, it is not very surprising that the goddess Brigid had her feast day at this point. She was a goddess of the hearth fire, poetry, smithcraft, healing, and fertility. She rekindled the fire in the earth, preparing it for the reemergence of the living green plants. Fire to the Celts had many meanings. It was the source of heat and the central point of the home. It was a source of inspiration and divination. It was also the power used in smithcraft, for the fire heated the metal and made it soft enough to work. All of these things were in Brigid's domain. In addition, she was a patron of fosterage. This was a Celtic custom whereby children would be raised by different adults in the community. In later times, when the Christian Saint Brigid took on much of the goddess's role, she was given the title of Foster Mother of Jesus. She kept many of the same attributes as the goddess Brigid. This early spring festival is also called "Brigid" or "Brigit," as her association with the themes of the day was so important, her name became synonymous with celebration itself.

Much that was done at this festival dealt with the early stages of life (plant, animal, and human) and how this new life was important to the overall domestic life of the tribe.

Plowing the land

Badgers and other local animals see their shadows

New green grass

A woman in the village or house, representing the goddess Brigid, blessed household fires, food remaining after winter, the smith's forge, and farming tools

New lambs born

Early spring flowers

New life around the farm yard

23

Lughnasa—Around August 1
The Beginning of the Harvest

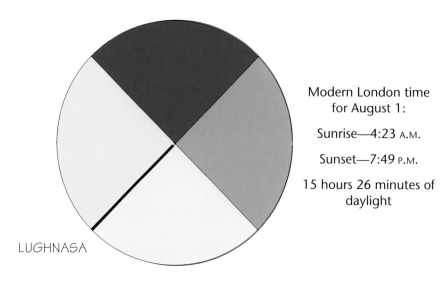

LUGHNASA

Modern London time for August 1:

Sunrise—4:23 A.M.

Sunset—7:49 P.M.

15 hours 26 minutes of daylight

Lughnasa falls exactly opposite Imbolc, and halfway between Beltane and Samhain. It marks the halfway point in the light side of the year.

This was a celebration of the beginning of the harvest, and a celebration of Lugh, an Irish sun god. As the sun is at its strongest in the summer, it is an appropriate time to celebrate its life-giving energy. Lughnasa was a time of great joy, as the first harvest had been brought in. One of the old Irish mythological tales says that at the beginning of the harvest season, the trickster god, Lugh, wins control of the fruits of the soil from the earth giants and turns them over to the human community. He is associated with lightning and with the storms that cool the air after the worst of the season's heat. The name *Lammas* is an Anglo-Saxon word for the same festival. Several cities in Britain and Northern Europe are named after Lugh; London, England, and Lyons, France, are but two.

To the early Anglo-Saxons, this seasonal festival was called *Hlafmas* or "Loafmass," as this was when grains of barley, wheat, and rye were ripening. In celebration, loaves of bread were baked and shared among families and communities. Other foods grown then were a form of corn, various types of turnips, carrots, onions, and perhaps lettuces. Wild fruits (like apples and berries) and nuts were collected in season.

Lughnasa marked when the fall harvest was begun. Shepherds started to bring cattle, sheep, and goats in from higher pastures, while the preparing, counting, settling, drying, and storing of food for the winter survival began. Everyone available in the villages was called out to help with the harvest. Although days were growing shorter, the sun could still be hot in Britain and northern Europe.

In ancient Ireland, a great celebration was held in honor of Lugh's foster mother, and attendance was required by law.

Today, in parts of Britain, there are still harvest fairs and village dancing when the major part of the harvest is in. There are many old

stories about a newcomer who defeats an unpopular lord in a contest of strength or skill held during a harvest festival. The British harvest festivities included games that paralleled those stories. They held contests whose winner would be crowned "lord" for the following year, only to be challenged by another "newcomer" at the next year's harvest festival. Many of these stories are kept alive in mummers plays, which are still performed today.

In Scotland, Highland Games are still held in mid- to late summer.

Druid priests light fires in honor of Celtic sun god Lugh

Harvest fairs, village dancing, feasting, contests, music

Returning of livestock from summer pastures

Drying racks for fish, meats, fruits

Contests of strength

Food purchasing, storing, and preparing for winter

Buying and selling of livestock

Equinoxes and Solstices

Although the Celts were certainly aware of the solstices (the shortest and longest days of the year) and the equinoxes (when day and night are of equal length in fall and spring), and probably used them to reckon events, as far as we know they did not attach major celebrations to them.

Most of the celebrations we see for the equinoxes come primarily from other cultures such as the Norse and the Romans. The Vikings, in all likelihood, brought both solstice and equinox celebrations to the Celts, and the later invasions by Germanic tribes into Britain helped solidify the customs. Even though the early Celts didn't pay much attention to the equinoxes, virtually every other culture in the world celebrated these days. As the Celts traded with the rest of the world, they surely were aware that the equinoxes were significant days for other peoples.

The solstices marked key turning points in the year. The winter solstice—the shortest, darkest day of the year—nevertheless marks the victory of light over darkness, holding the promise of more light to come, as the days begin to grow longer from that day on. Likewise, the summer solstice—the longest day of the year—marks the victory of darkness over light, as the days begin to grow shorter from that day on. *Festivals held to mark these days seemed to be less agricultural in theme and more in the realm of the sacred and magical.* Some cultures thought the winter solstice was more

important than the summer solstice, and others thought just the opposite. But, throughout the world, the mystical rising and setting of the sun and the seasonal lengthening and shortening of the days has been held in awe as sacred and magical.

The solstices were noted by observing the rising and setting of the sun. When the sun rose or set in the same place for several days, its rising (or setting) point seemed to stand still. Many of the great stone circles in Great Britain and western France are aligned to the solstices, so that the sun rises and sets over particular stones at those times. There are also many sacred buildings and caves around the world (Canyon de Chelly and Chaco Canyon in the United States, for example) that are likewise aligned. At a particular moment, (for example, noon on the summer solstice), the sun will form a pattern on a particular place on the wall. These places tend to be marked with sacred drawings or symbols. As the solstices celebrated the cycles of life and death within all creation, it was usually the spiritual leaders of the community—the priests, priestesses, or shamans—who announced them and were the central figures in solstice ceremonies.

Sunrise light on Winter Solstice

Constructed around 3200 BC, the massive mound of rocks at Newgrange in Ireland encloses a tomb beneath. At sunrise (8:58 AM) on the winter solstice a shaft of light beams deeply through a carefully designed opening into the inner chamber, momentarily illuminating the darkness within. To ancient peoples, the annual reassurance that light would return to overcome the darkness was important enough to erect such a huge monument. And there are others throughout the world.

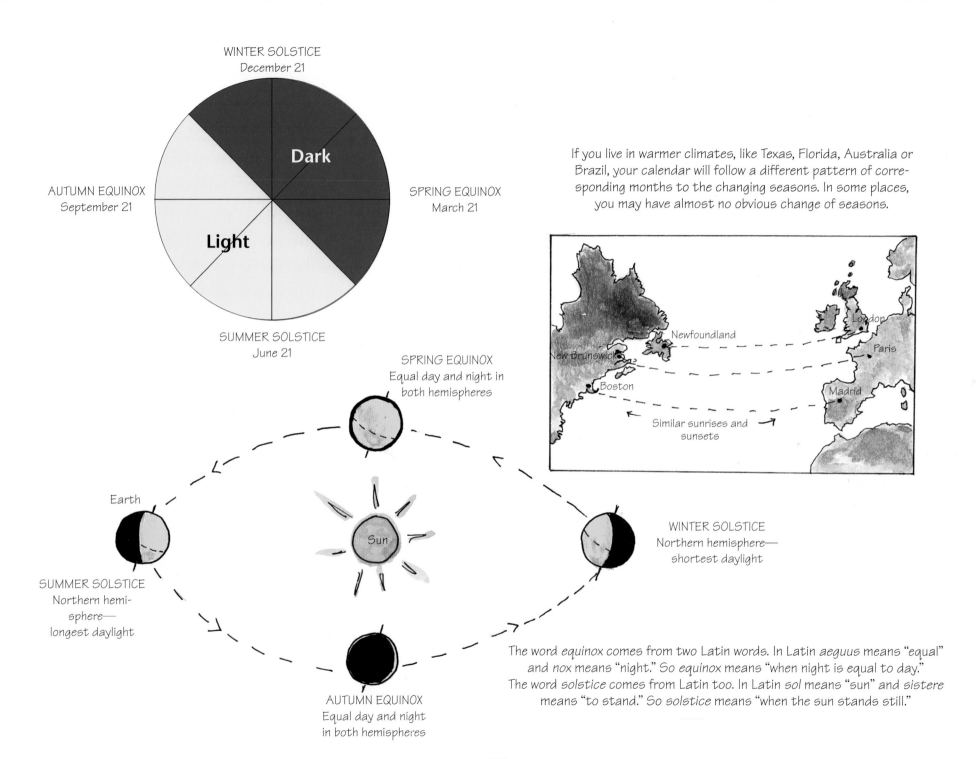

WINTER SOLSTICE
December 21

Dark

AUTUMN EQUINOX
September 21

SPRING EQUINOX
March 21

Light

SUMMER SOLSTICE
June 21

If you live in warmer climates, like Texas, Florida, Australia or Brazil, your calendar will follow a different pattern of corresponding months to the changing seasons. In some places, you may have almost no obvious change of seasons.

Newfoundland

New Brunswick

London

Paris

Boston

Madrid

Similar sunrises and sunsets

SPRING EQUINOX
Equal day and night in both hemispheres

Earth

Sun

WINTER SOLSTICE
Northern hemisphere—shortest daylight

SUMMER SOLSTICE
Northern hemisphere—longest daylight

AUTUMN EQUINOX
Equal day and night in both hemispheres

The word *equinox* comes from two Latin words. In Latin *aeguus* means "equal" and *nox* means "night." So equinox means "when night is equal to day." The word *solstice* comes from Latin too. In Latin *sol* means "sun" and *sistere* means "to stand." So *solstice* means "when the sun stands still."

27

The Winter Solstice—December 20–22
(varies astronomically every year)

WINTER SOLSTICE

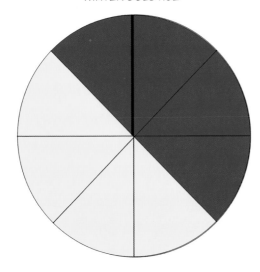

At the winter solstice, the Celts made final preparations for the coming winter. Any of the livestock that were not being used for breeding or would not be needed in the spring, were slaughtered for food. The Celts would salt the meat to last through the winter. Fresh meat was only enjoyed in the late fall and early wintertime, as were fresh fruits and vegetables that would not last in storage. The feasting around the winter solstice celebrated the bounty of the land and often led to excess. As the year was filled with hard work just prior to the solstice and not much work immediately after (crops were already harvested, the ground was frozen, and animals had been slaughtered) there was plenty of time for lengthy celebrations.

The Roman festival of world renewal was called Saturnalia, with its feasting, drinking, and wild celebrations. This was the most important holiday in pre-Christian Rome. It came just before the winter solstice and was followed by the New Year. (At a later point, the New Year was celebrated at the time of the spring equinox.)

In later medieval times, the celebrations of the winter solstice usually featured a "Lord of Misrule," who turned the standard social order upside down. The rich were treated as poor servants and the poor would be treated as rich. Men would dress as women and women dress as men. The workers would go to their lord and sing songs to gain entrance. Once inside the great homes of the ruling lords, they would be given the best food and drink. This is the origin of wassailing, and of our present-day tradition of caroling.

People lit sacred fires, kindled from a bonfire held sacred by the village, in their homes to drive away evil spirits. In Norse cultures, the sacred fires involved a Yule log and were burned indoors.

Yule comes from the old Anglo-Saxon word *geola*, meaning "yoke" (of the year). At Yuletide, the sun is caught at its lowest point in the sky, but only briefly. For in the celebration of Yule we find rebirth, new growth, and the survival of light in the darkness. This was a celebration of the sun, despite the dark season. In this darkest time of the year, to keep the balance and maintain hope, people celebrated the sun.

Mistletoe, which grows on oaks, a tree sacred to the Celts, is a symbol of eternal life. Cut by a druid in a ritual ceremony, great bunches of mistletoe were hung in doorways in Brittany (in France) at the winter solstice to ensure good fortune for their homes. There are overlaps between celebrations of the winter solstice, Yule, Saturnalia, and Christmas. When Christianity began to spread it made sense for the early Christians to place Christ's birth at the same time as the solstice. Linking the birth of God's son with the annual birth of the celestial sun held a strong appeal for both Christians and non-Christians in the common metaphor of the birth of Light.

The Summer King slays the Winter King, symbolizing summer's coming return.

29

The Spring Equinox—March 20–22 (varies astronomically every year)

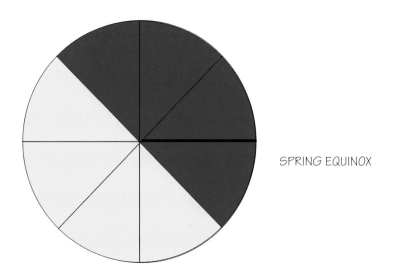

SPRING EQUINOX

From Imbolc to Beltane, we have the season of spring. After the long, dark winter, people all over the world love to celebrate spring. From Valentine's Day and Mardi Gras to spring equinox, Easter, and May Day celebrations, many of our modern celebrations have roots in older traditions. As winter slowly turned to summer, people in ancient times were concerned about the year's harvest. The fertility of the land and of the people in their family was very important. Many of these celebrations stem from ancient rites to ensure a fruitful year, both in the fields and in the home.

The Celts would plant their crops by mid-March. In late March and early April, they got their livestock ready for the migration to upper pastures. In late April, they would hoe the crops to give them the best growing conditions, and in mid- to late May they would thin them so their main crops could grow bigger and stronger.

On February 15, the Romans celebrated the Feast of Februata Juno, mother of the gods. It was customary at this time for men and women

to divine who their future loves would be. Names of girls were written on pieces of paper that boys would blindly choose. The Catholic Church tried to change these customs by declaring the day Saint Valentine's Day (supposedly Saint Valentine was martyred on February 14 in A.D. 271). Rather than picking girls' names, boys were encouraged to draw the names of saints to be studied and emulated on that day. This idea, obviously, did not catch on.

Among parents in medieval Ireland, the entire forty days of Lent was a time of matchmaking . Weddings were set to follow Easter. This seems to be part of a long tradition which predates the Christian holy days.

Masks were worn in spring celebrations to frighten away the winter demons and spirits, while hiding the identity of the wearer. People wearing masks and costumes, and carrying lit torches, would run through the streets screaming and yelling. Mummers parades and carnivals are modern descendants of this tradition. Mardi Gras, a great party that happens in New Orleans and much of Latin America every year just before Lent, comes

the egg is source of new life, it is no surprise to see these traditions merged into our present one where the Easter Bunny delivers gaily decorated Easter eggs. Eggs were not eaten during Lent (in the Catholic Church) but they were the main feature of the Easter meal. The name Easter comes from the names of the goddesses, Ishtar (Babylonian), Astarte (Phoenician), Eostre (Saxon), and Eos (Roman), whose aspects had to do with spring and dawn.

In the old Roman calendar, where there were only ten months, Easter and the spring equinox once marked the beginning of the new year.

directly from this European tradition of Carneval. These parades were also funeral parades for the "dead" winter.

Plowing the land to prepare for the growth of the crops was supposed to have magical powers in fertility rites. Traditions in many northern European countries suggest that an unmarried woman who draws the plow, or even sits on it, will be married soon and have healthy children. Rain was crucial to the success of the crops, so water had a special importance.

Another fertility rite was the "rod of life." Branches were broken off a young bush, and anyone touched by them would be blessed with good health and fertility. This tradition is carried on today in many European carnivals, where young women are tapped with the decorated branches of the pussy willow. This also shows the ancient roots of the symbolism behind catching the bridal bouquet at a wedding (being touched by the rod of life) and being the next to marry.

The Easter Bunny, too, has its roots in ancient traditions. The rabbit's fertility is legendary and as

31

The Summer Solstice—June 20–22 (varies astronomically every year)

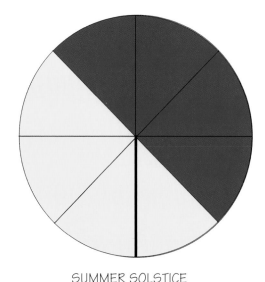

SUMMER SOLSTICE

This was the time of sheep shearing and the harvesting of wool. This was also the time to breed the cattle in order to ensure birthing of calves the next spring and to make hay, a real necessity to feed the animals during non-growing months. In order to survive the winter, the Celts developed storage capabilities for large amounts of food (sealed storage pits), both for themselves and for their animals.

In addition to cattle and sheep, the Celts' livestock also included goats, pigs (domestic and wild), and horses. The horses helped make the Celts a warrior aristocracy, and were probably not used as farming labor; oxen would have been used instead.

Many of the great megalithic stone circles, such as Stonehenge, are oriented to sunrise at the summer solstice. As this is common throughout Europe, and indeed, throughout the Northern Hemisphere, this suggests that the summer solstice was very important to cultures long before the time of the Celts. There isn't much evidence

to show how the Celts observed the solstices in ways that were culturally their own. There is little mention of the solstices or equinoxes in the myths and legends or in the writings we have translated today.

The summer solstice was a festival of the earth. For, while the sun was high in the sky and the weather was warm, it was important to maintain balance. Just as the winter solstice was a celebration of the sun in the dark period, a joyous occasion in a dark time, the summer solstice was a celebration that had a sadness to it. It was the beginning of the decline of the sun, and though it was a time of abundance, there was need to be aware of winter's shortages. An ancient proverb from Cornwall, England, says *"yn ha, porth kov a wav,"* which means "In summer, remember winter."

Midsummer Day was also a day to gather herbs to cure fever and combat diseases. Herbs such as vervain, echinacea, and St. John's wort were all collected at this time.

- A hazel rod cut at the summer solstice was thought to be a fine divining rod.

- In Denmark and Norway, fires were burned to banish disease from cattle.

- Cowherds in Scotland would carry torches around their folds to purify and protect them.

- The dying light of the sun meant a defeat of the Summer King, who would fight the Winter King every solstice. Their rivalry would continue throughout the year.

The summer solstice rites appear forgotten, merged into the Christian feasts of Saint John the Baptist and The Assumption.

The Winter King slays the Summer King, symbolizing winter's coming return.

The Autumn Equinox—September 20–22 (varies astronomically every year)

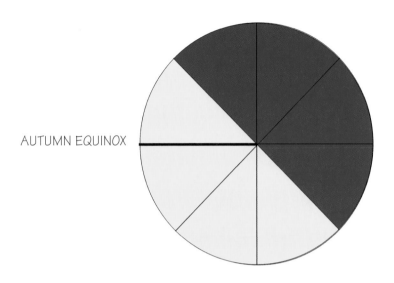

AUTUMN EQUINOX

Much of the work of preparing for the winter months was done around the fall equinox (September 21). Once the grains (mainly wheat and barley, though rye, oats, and millet were also grown) and hay had been brought in from the fields to the settlement, they would be prepared for storage. The grains would be separated into categories: storage, immediate consumption, seeds for next year, and hops for beer. The grains that were to be stored would be prepared and placed in large storage pits, to be used in the winter for breads, porridge, stews, and beer. Beer, a drink dating back many centuries, was much loved by the Romans, who were known for their wine. They traded Roman wine to the Celts for Celtic beer!

The livestock were turned out in the fields to clear the remaining grain and to manure the soil for the coming year's crops. The farm livestock were mostly goats, pigs, sheep, cattle, and oxen.

Another time-consuming fall activity was clearing the forests (which in both continental Europe and Britain were once large and extensive). People needed timber in great quantities to build the round or oblong houses in which the Celts lived. The fencing around a village would use three hundred trees. A modest house (of which there were many in a village) would require one hundred trees and a large round house would use two hundred trees.* Thatching for a roof on a large round house required fifteen to twenty tons of thatching straw. A great deal of time and energy was needed to construct these villages. With all this work going on at this time of year, and with the Lughnasa celebrations just passed, it's easy to imagine why the Celts didn't hold big festivals at the autumn equinox.

---

*Many Celtic villages had a large round house for the chieftain and a number of smaller round houses for the rest of the clan.

Hunting of woodland animals

Abundant timber in the great forests of Europe

Livestock sent to fields to clear remaining crops

Oats

Rye

Wheat

Barley

Millet

35

Part III
Modern Ways to Celebrate the Ancient Festivals

The festivals just described came out of traditions begun long, long ago—as much as 2,700 years ago! As peoples moved to different lands and took on differing religions and customs, these festivals changed and evolved. But they are still celebrated at the same times of the year.

- Samhain became the Christian celebration of All Saints' and All Souls' Days. All Saints' Day was also known as All Hallows' Day (*hallow* is Old English for saint, a hallowed person). These celebrations evolved into a three-day festival with All Hallows' Eve (Halloween) celebrated on October 31, All Saints' Day celebrated on November 1, and All Souls' Day on November 2.

- Imbolc became the Christian Candlemas and the folk legend of Groundhog Day, set on February 2.

- Beltane became a general spring festival, May Day, and Lady Day, in honor of the Virgin Mary, set on May 1.

- Lughnasa became a countryside celebration of the harvest, set with Saint John's Day on August 1.

In colonial America, the Puritans banned these festivals because of their non-Christian origins. With the large Irish immigrations in the 1840s, the Old World Celtic traditions began to seep back into the culture of those living in the New World. Today, with the increased commercialization of these celebrations, it can be difficult to determine exactly what has been done traditionally and what is part of our modern culture. We will talk about the modern celebrations in the same order that we talked about Samhain, Beltane, Imbolc, and Lughnasa to remind ourselves of their Celtic origins and of what was important to the Celts, the division of the year into dark and light, winter and summer (see page 15).

Halloween (Samhain—October 31)

All Hallows' Eve, or Halloween, comes from the early Christian adaptation of the most important festival of the Celtic Year, Samhain. Sometime after A.D. 400, All Hallows' Eve was spent in church praying for the souls of the dead. November 1 and November 2 were spent visiting the graves of the dead. In Spanish-speaking cultures in North, Central, and South America, *El Dia de los Muertos* (The Day of the Dead) is celebrated on November 2, with whole families spending the night in cemeteries to honor the souls of their ancestors. In Italy, the Roman festival of Pomona, the goddess of fruits, was celebrated around November 1, with similar overlaps in customs to the celebration of Samhain by their neighbors to the north.

In the ninth century A.D., Pope Gregory IV placed All Saints' Day and All Hallows' Eve in the church calendar. Increasingly, throughout medieval Europe and here in the colonies of early America, all celebrations on October 31 that were not church related were condemned. But in rural areas in Ireland, Scotland, Wales, and parts of England, folk customs continued well into the twentieth century. It is some of these folk traditions that we describe on the following page. Our customs of trick-or-treating and Mischief Night pranks come from folk culture.

Witches did not exist in the early Celtic cultures. The word witch comes from an old Anglo-Saxon word, "Wicca," meaning wizard. In early cultures wizards, sorcerers, druids, shamans, and witches were wise advisors of a community who understood the rhythms and mysteries of life in the world of nature. Witches were associated with Halloween by the Medieval Church as they celebrated the Celtic Year's End festival of Samhain. Witches could be young, old, pretty, ugly. Often they helped the sick and delivered babies.

- Locate sunrise and sunset times for your area. Compare with Beltane times.

Bonfires were lit on hilltops to ward off evil spirits out stealing milk, destroying the crops, and harming livestock.
Pranksters and mischief makers roamed countrysides dressed in costumes playing tricks on neighbors. Blame was placed on "spirits" abroad.

Trickster—the countryside prankster Similar costumes are still worn at Mardi Gras in America and at Carneval in Europe.

Costumes worn to scare away evil spirits

* Light an orange candle. Blow it out. Think of all the fires extinguished and relit over the ages to honor the year's end. Relight one hour later as a sign that the New Year has begun.

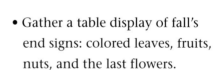

- Cut apples in cross section to float in hot cider, a drink common in Medieval Europe. Find the five-pointed star, an ancient symbol of the Goddess and protection.

Trick or treat evolved from an Irish custom of groups of peasants going from house to house asking for money and food in the name of Muck Olla, an Irish god, and later, in the name of Saint Columba, a sixth-century priest.

Candles put in rutabagas to scare away spirits—today we use pumpkins.

- Gather a table display of fall's end signs: colored leaves, fruits, nuts, and the last flowers.

- Leave a saucer of milk out for the faerie folk or spirits abroad—to please them.

May Day (Beltane—May 1)

In many communities, people are bringing back the traditions of the Celtic past, especially where the customs were the last to leave. You might want to investigate May Day fairs, parades, pageants (such as the Spring Revels), maypole dancing, and morris dancing in or near your local community. In Minehead, Padstow, and Helston, England, May Day festivals and pageants are still held in the towns' streets every year.

During the ancient festival, cattle would be driven between two fires to purify and protect them from disease before they were sent out to the pastures. In many villages of Celtic ancestry, this purification practice is still held.

In Ireland, the months before Beltane were when marriages were planned. There was much matchmaking among the adults of each clan or tribe, and weddings would be held at Beltane. Couples would leap over the sacred fire to ensure fertility in their marriage. Today, late spring marriages are still popular, especially in June.

In May Day celebrations, washing your face in the early morning dew is said to have magical consequences. The first man seen by a woman who had just washed her face in the dew would be her lover or future husband.

The crowning of the May Queen also derives from old Celtic traditions. She would represent the Flower Maiden or the young aspect of the Goddess. Christian tradition has absorbed this with the crowning with flowers of statues of the Virgin Mary on May Day. Today we also have festivals to crown the "Queen of the May" and Mother's Day and May Day picnics as well.

A fair maid, who, the first of May
Goes to the fields at break of day
And washed in dew 'neath the hawthorn tree
will ever after handsome be
—Traditional rhyme

Children in some English villages still celebrate May Day with fairs and dancing outdoors.

38

• Locate sunrise and sunset times for your area. Compare with Samhain times.

• Find a small tree or shrub and decorate its newly leafing branches with colored ribbons or strips of cloth. This tradition is still found in Cornwall and Ireland as a request for healing and renewal by spring's energy.

• Find a time during your day to go outdoors and sit in a quiet place. Be really quiet for 3–5 minutes. Then write: three sounds, three colors, three images of new spring. Make a short poem or a three-sentence description using those observations. Now pretend you are part of a tree, leaf, cloud, or flying bird. The Celts were known for their ability to "shape shift"—that is to take on the form of the animals around them.

• To make a dandelion chain, slit each stem and insert the next.

• In many communities, people are bringing back traditions of the Celtic past. Investigate a local May Day Fair, maypole, sword, or morris dancing.

• Make some hard-boiled eggs, then save the water you boiled them in. Put it outside for the Faeries.

• Investigate stories about Faeries, such as Tam Lin or the story of Thomas The Rhymer.

Groundhog Day (Imbolc— February 2)

In northern New England, lambs are born in February so they will be ready to go to pasture with the adult sheep in summer.

In Europe, country people tired of the lingering winter would go out looking for signs of spring. For some unknown reason, someone latched onto the badger and decided the length of its shadow would determine spring's arrival. When Germans came to America, there were no celebrations on February 1, and badgers could not be found. A very sleepy and grumpy groundhog was chosen as the American substitute. The groundhog today still wonders: Why all the fuss on February 2? Any honest groundhog is in deep hibernation and won't awaken for another two months! In this case, myth and nature don't coordinate, until you go back to the source of the myth.

There is an old song from the Highlands of Scotland that talks about pounding the ground with a stick to bring forth the snake (who *doesn't* get pounded!) around the time of Imbolc. The behavior of the snake is thought to determine the remaining period of frost. The snake has long been associated with wealth and treasure. Could there be a parallel between the appearance of the snake from underground, bringing omens of wealth and treasure, and the groundhog on Groundhog Day, bringing the treasure of an early spring and growing season?

To see a hedgehog on this day is a herald of good planting weather."
—Old Irish saying

In the Roman Catholic Church, Imbolc has become Candlemas, the day that candles are blessed for the coming year in Mary's honor. An old Scottish rhyme about Candlemas ties in with our Groundhog Day mythology that a sunny day will mean six more weeks of winter, while a cloudy day portends an early spring. (If you count six weeks from February 2, you actually come to the spring equinox on March 20, 21, or 22!)

If Candlemas be fair and bright
Come winter have another flight.
If Candlemas brings clouds and rain
Go winter and come not again.

Saint Brigid's Day and Candlemas have come to be celebrated around the same time and come from two different streams of culture. Brigid is one of the names of an ancient Celtic goddess and Saint Brigid is a Christian saint whose story borrows many parts from the older goddess's stories. This mixture of Christian with pre-Christian material is quite common. She is remembered today as Saint Brigid of Kildare. The nuns of Saint Brigid kept a fire burning continuously from early times to the 1500s when Henry VIII destroyed most of the abbeys in Britain. In the early Christian church, church leaders decided that this day should also commemorate the day when Mary's parents took her to the temple for purification. Celtic tradition holds that Saint Brigid went with her, and the event is celebrated by the feast of Candlemas.

As Christianity spread throughout Europe, it absorbed many local customs and replaced them with its own. This was possible because there were many similarities between Christianity and the local agricultural religions. The later use of force against the Celts was more about the political aspects of Christianity than about differences in spiritual beliefs.

At Candlemas, Saint Brigid's cross is still placed on doors for protection today.

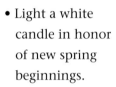

• Pour a small cup of milk or cream on the ground in honor of Imbolc and to thank the earth for feeding us through the winter's cold.

• On a sunny day, stand outdoors, facing the sun (close your eyes!). Open your eyes and look to see where and how long your shadow is. You can determine the time of day and the time of year this way.

In North America, woodchucks are still in full hibernation and will not awaken for two months.

• Light a white candle in honor of new spring beginnings.

• Collect branches of pussy willow, forsythia, or apple. Put in water and watch them grow flowers and leaves.

• Locate sunrise and sunset times for your region. Compare with Samhain times. Notice longer daylight since December 21!

• Look for signs of spring coming in your area: swelling buds on trees, snowdrops, crocuses, aconite in bloom.

—Birds begin spring calls—finches, chickadees, jays, owls, cardinals, titmice.

—Roads turn from ice to mud.

—The white of snowdrops is a symbol of newness and transformation from dark winter to the light of spring.

Harvest Festivals (Lughnasa—August 1)

Many different cultures in the Northern Hemisphere held Sun festivals and early harvest festivals to honor the now waning sun and the full production of the harvest season. In Scotland, Highland Games are still held in mid- to late summer.

Various North, Central, and South American tribes have annual corn festivals, sun festivals, harvest festivals, and other social gatherings to join people together before the cold of the next season sets in.

The Catholic churches of Britain have turned this agricultural festival into a religious one—Loaf Mass, when the loaves containing grain from the first harvest are brought into churches and blessed.

For farmers and countryfolk, this was often the busiest time of the year. Haying was in full swing. Garden crops such as beans, onions, lettuce, and turnips were being picked. Wild fruits and berries were gathered. Woodland animals and lake or ocean fish were hunted throughout the summer. Often the work became communal, bringing families together to harvest the grains, construct new buildings, and repair pasture walls. Picnics and fairs evolved into 4H fairs, county fairs, and so on.

In Britain, during early August, there once was a public holiday called "Wakes Week" where as many townsfolk as possible left their daily jobs to help with the harvesting. Today this has survived as the Bank Holiday Monday at the end of August.

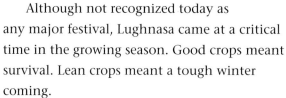

Although not recognized today as any major festival, Lughnasa came at a critical time in the growing season. Good crops meant survival. Lean crops meant a tough winter coming.

Later, after corn was introduced to Britain from the New World, tradition had it that from the last stalks of the best corn, dollies should be made. These would be placed over the hearth in British homes all winter. Come spring, the seeds would be shaken out and added to the new year's planting. (Corn dollies and woven ornaments are still made in Sweden today.)

Harvest Corn Bread

Corn came to the Celtic countries from the New World.

$^3/_4$ cup flour
$2^1/_2$ teaspoons baking powder
$^3/_4$ teaspoon salt
$1^1/_2$ cups cornmeal
1 teaspoon cinnamon
1 egg
$1^1/_2$ tablespoons honey
3 tablespoons melted butter or oil

Preheat oven to 475°F. Grease a 6" x 3" loaf pan, a 9" x 9" baking pan, or a muffin tin. In a large bowl, mix the dry ingredients together, then add the wet. Stir to combine. Bake for 25 minutes or until golden brown.

Dry August and warm
Doth harvest no harm
—Sixteenth-century verse

Singing insects of summer

Bush katydids

Field crickets

Short-horned grasshoppers

Harvest Festival–Lughnasa Activities

- Locate sunrise and sunset times and compare them with Samhain.

- Find an area near you where people still harvest hay for feeding livestock through the winter. In early Celtic times, three cuttings of hay was crucial to winter survival. In New England today, farmers usually make no more than two cuts.

- Take a warm summer night's walk, preferably away from lights and noise. How many natural sounds do you hear—crickets, grasshoppers, birds, animals, rustling leaves?

- Imagine you are living 2,500 years ago. Could you hear some of the same sounds, see some of the same stars, and see the same moon?

- Gather garden and wildflowers to make a Lughnasa wreath. Make the circle backing firm by using bittersweet, wild grape, or willow. (Do not use poison ivy!) Add cross pieces to signify the four Celtic festivals.

The Wheel

We have seen how we can draw a circle and use it to represent a set of observable events, like the cycle of the seasons. This allows us to use it as a calendar of a sort. The wheel can also function as a map. For example, we can place north on the top of the circle, like a compass. East falls to the right, south below, and west on the left. This example can be expanded to become a simple observational map of the entire visible universe simply by expanding the circle or wheel into a three-dimensional sphere. With yourself in the center, above you are all the things you see in the sky. Below you is what's under you, and the directions are all around you.

By combining the directions of the land with the seasons of the year on our wheel, we expand the wheel another way. For example, in northern Europe, the north was cold and the south was hot. So, we put winter in the north and summer in the south. This follows the dark/light arrangement as well. Following the natural cycle of the seasons, spring goes into the east and autumn goes in the west.

We could continue to add more and more to this wheel. Your wheel can contain many different events. If you were to make a true observational calendar, you might include events like:

- The first robin you see

- The first baseball game you see

- When you see leaves return to a tree in your yard

- When you first see those leaves turn color

- The first snowfall of the season you see

If you live in a place where tourism is very important, you might list the first tourist you spot arriving, and the last tourist to leave. This would mark the tourist season.

You don't need to limit yourself to a perceived year, the wheel works well as a map of any period of time. The hours of the day on our clocks are a variation on this idea.

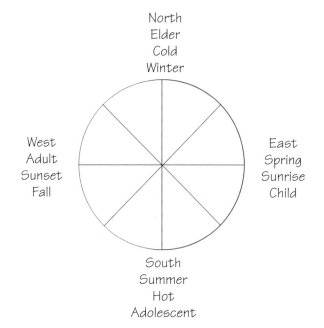

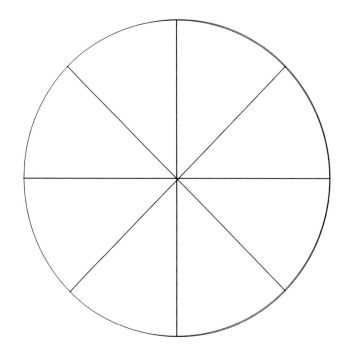

Create your own calendar wheel

44

Raven is my brother.

Crow is my sister.

The fast waters by

my house wash me

and the Sun dries me.

To summer I give my energy.

To fall I give my preparations.

To winter I give my rest.

To spring I give my rebirth.

The turning year's wheel

teaches me the eternal cycles of life.

And I am thankful

for this year and that.

—Clare Walker Leslie

Poetry, song, dance, and stories are also ways of connecting
with the cycles of the seasons—both ancient and modern.

Part IV
How Natural Science Explains Ancient Traditions

The ancient peoples studied changes in the sun, moon, and stars and guided their growing year, their travels, their celebrations, their battles, and their politics according to these heavenly signs. Although the Celts did not call themselves scientists, they did rely upon observation of natural events to better understand their world.

The Moon Cycle

Many cultures celebrated festivals at evening moonrise. The Celts determined their quarterly festivals using the phases of the moon. The moon's cycle was a reliable measure of time. It always took twenty-nine days to go from dark to dark or full to full. The moon would be in the same phase over all the Celtic lands at any given time.

Because these cycles corresponded with a woman's monthly cycle of fertility, many early people regarded the moon as a goddess.

The cycles of the moon also affect the tides on Earth. When the moon's gravitational pull is strongest, we have high tides. When it is weak, we have low tides. Because the Celts and many other ancient peoples were sailors, knowledge of the tides and the phases of the moon was an important aspect of their understanding of the world they lived in, and of the many different levels of interaction between the Earth, the sun, the moon, and the stars.

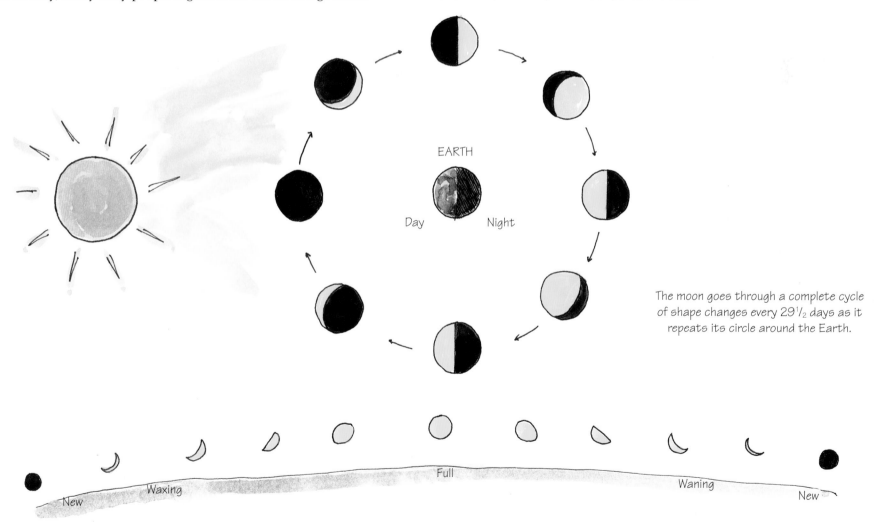

EARTH

Day   Night

The moon goes through a complete cycle of shape changes every 29½ days as it repeats its circle around the Earth.

New   Waxing   Full   Waning   New

47

Anywhere you live, you can see where the sun sets behind the land, you can observe how the sun "moves" across the sky, from season to season, increasing and decreasing its "time" in the sky as it goes.

As the Earth turns in its 365-day path around the sun, it appears that the sun is moving slowly north and south in the sky, thus giving us our seasons.

SPRING

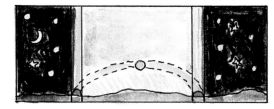

Begins March 20–21–22
Equal day and night in
both hemispheres

Shadow directions
change too as
seasons change

Sun rises and sets
due E and due W
on Spring Equinox

SUMMER

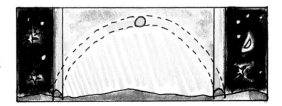

Begins June 20–21–22
Longest days in
Northern hemisphere
Shortest days in
Southern hemisphere

Sun rises and sets
far NE and far NW
on Summer Solstice

FALL

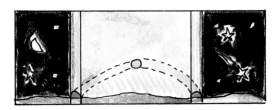

Begins September 20–21–22
Equal day and night in
both hemispheres

Sun rises and sets
due E and due W
on Autumn Equinox

WINTER

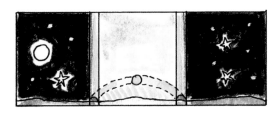

Begins December 20–21–22
Shortest days in Northern
hemisphere
Longest days in Southern
hemisphere

Sun rises and sets
far SE and SW on
the Winter Solstice

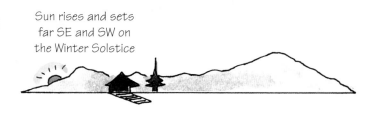

The Constellations

At night, the stars and groups of stars—called constellations—guided ancient people as they traveled. In the Northern Hemisphere, people would use the Pole Star to determine their whereabouts. When they faced the Pole Star they knew they were facing north. Today, sailors still position their routes at night by the stars.

As the earth moved through the months, so the patterns of the stars changed. Knowing what stars were visible during the different times of the year was very valuable knowledge. To help with this, stars were grouped into constellations and given names by astronomers. They created stories and myths to explain what otherwise could not be understood, for example, why some constellations seemed to move more than others.

It is now thought that the large star the three magi, or the three wise men, followed west to find the Christ child was either a spectacular comet or a combination of Mars, Jupiter, and Saturn. (These wise men were from the land of Persia, where the word for priest or wizard was, in fact, *magus* or, in plural, *magi*. It is also believed these ancient priests, astronomers, and wizards were our first scientists.)

What stories do you know about the constellations?

Pole Star or North Star

Little Dipper or Little Bear

Taurus the Bull

Seven Sisters or Pleiades

Orion and his Belt

Cassiopeia and her Chair

These constellations have names from Greek mythologies. Other cultures have their own names.

Ways of Telling Time and Keeping Records

Many cultures used a variety of ways to tell the passage of time or to record important events. Before handwriting developed, people kept records by making marks, drawing pictures, or erecting huge stone monuments.

We think that the existing standing stones found in Brittany, Scotland, Ireland, Wales, and England were built to mark four seasonal changes: two solstices and two equinoxes. Ancient people, between 4000 and 2000 B.C., built these giant stone monuments, like Stonehenge in England, to observe the precise rising and setting of the sun at the solstices and equinoxes. (Unfortunately, over time farmers have used a number of the standing stones for walls and buildings, so we don't know how many there once were.) The Great Pyramids of Egypt were built later than the oldest stone circles, between 2600 and 2400 B.C.

notches on sticks

herd counts—
spirals on rock walls
or on animal hides

paintings on rock
walls of caves

accounts of animal
hunts or spirit
journeys

sun dials

How would you tell time if
you had no clock?

standing stones

You can use your own
shadow to figure time
and season.

High noon

Late afternoon or
early evening

Part V
Where Do Traditions and Calendars Come From?

What we call folk traditions exist in every country. These traditions are made up of stories, songs, dances, styles of dress, particular festivals, and ways of speaking. They tell the story of a group of people over time. Folk history is part fact and part myth, as it often mixes the stories of tribal heroes with gods and goddesses. Sometimes we call these stories mythic history. They have usually been told out loud for many, many years before ever being written down.

What makes a group of people behave in similar ways? One important factor is the climate. People who live in a very cold climate have different customs from people who live in the tropics. And in cultures with seasonal changes there are special customs for each season.

Different songs are sung in the winter than in the summer. We dress lightly for hot weather, wear more festive colors in the spring, and tell different stories in the rain than we would when it's bright and sunny. Over time, a group of people usually develops a collection of traditional songs and stories that they sing and tell at the same time each year. If two groups live in similar climates, their stories will be more alike than stories from very different environments.

Many ancient tribes had close relationships with their land. It provided them with food and shelter. It was very important for them to understand how to work with nature in order to survive. If the hunting was bad or if the crops didn't grow, there would be no food. When the conditions were favorable, they lived well. People who lived in hot desert regions learned different survival techniques from those who lived in cooler, forested regions or tropical, wet regions. So of course their songs and stories were different too, reflecting their varied experiences. The story of the land was a big part of the story of the early people.

Their stories, songs, and dances included important information about how to live in their homelands: what crops to plant, and when and where to plant them; who the best hunters were, how they hunted, and where. This knowledge became part of their tradition and was passed on from generation to generation, often becoming the main thing that held otherwise scattered communities together. People gathered at harvest times, planting times, and cattle trading times to celebrate. The culture grew as the stories, songs, and dances grew. New experiences meant new stories to add to the old ones.

People's stories and songs, clothing and customs change and grow over time to keep up with the experience of those whose story is being told. This is what we call a living tradition. Today we can look at the traditions of people from other places and see clues to how they once lived, what was important to them, what kinds of things happened to them, and how they reacted.

Sports events, dances, parties, and highland games at seasonal festival times are reminders of ancient village and tribal festivals.

The success of winter and summer
revels—or celebrations—around
the country indicates a true need
for revelry in America

Cultures can change peacefully when a group or tribe moves to a new land, and over time, the group adds its stories to those of the people who were there first. They can also change violently when one group of people invades the homeland of another and conquers them in battle. It's not uncommon for the winners to insist that their stories are the only stories people are allowed to tell. Sometimes, the conquered people keep telling their own stories to their children in secret to keep the old ways alive.

Except for the native peoples of North America, all Americans had relatives who once lived in another land or country. Do you know where your great grandfather grew up? Your great aunt? Your father?

Modern America is a great combination of many cultures, traditions, and celebrations. For over five hundred years, people from all over the world have been coming here to live, bringing with them the ways of the "Old Land"—Italy, India, Spain, France, China, Germany, Ireland, Africa—wherever their ancestors grew up.

But what does all this have to do with calendars? Well, imagine you and a small group of family members want to set a time to do something. You can use any number of different ways to define that time: the phases of the moon, where the sun is in the sky, when certain birds reappear after winter, when a certain tree loses its leaves. But what happens if you want to set a time to meet with someone who doesn't live in your village, and doesn't know your traditions? The phases of the moon are one good choice, because as long as people live in the same hemisphere they'll see the moon the same way at the same time. People need a way to mark time that is common to more groups than just those who live near them. As tribes met and traded with other tribes, whose growing seasons were a little different, these issues became more important. This is where the need for calendars began to take root. As tribes became villages and towns that traded with other towns, cities, and even countries, the need for a more sophisticated and universal way of keeping time grew.

When did people decide they needed a written calendar—a common way of keeping track of the passage of time?

The oldest documented calendar we know of dates back to 3000 B.C. in Egypt, where the annual flooding of the Nile's riverbanks determined the agricultural seasons. Although different countries and religions kept using their own calendars (and still do today), we have found records showing that the more populated regions of Europe were

Celtic religious beliefs are still
practiced in many Celtic Christian
homes as part of both Anglican
and Catholic beliefs

Eighth-century
Celtic cross

the first to use a calendar most like the international calendar commonly used today.

In 46 B.C., the Roman ruler Julius Caesar decided, with the advice of a Greek astronomer, that people could no longer use the moon to figure their calendar. A year's length, he said, had to do with the Sun's passage around the earth. He set twelve months of thirty to thirty-one days each (most named after Roman gods or warriors). Caesar's calendar was called the Julian calendar. It worked until 1582, when the Roman Catholic Pope Gregory XIII met with his astronomers and changed the Julian calendar to correct small errors. The Gregorian calendar is the Solar Calendar most in use today.

The Roman calendar, as we can see, was very much a political calendar. It celebrated the leaders of Rome and was based on ordering the days for the public observance of holidays and feasts. Rome was a big city, so the dates and events that city people wanted to remember and celebrate would naturally be different from the important dates of country people. The Celtic calendar was more of an agricultural calendar than a political one, marking the changing seasons and the key turning points of the year, when changes in climate affected the behavior of both people and animals. It also had religious aspects, in that its key festivals included underlying religious or spiritual themes. In earlier times, spiritual beliefs were more integrated into day-to-day living. Religious observances weren't separated off into churches and temples the way they often are today.

So, what exactly is the wheel of the year that we use to represent the

Calendar today? A circle, divided into eight equal segments, each marked by a day that defines the turning point of a season. These days are determined either by an astronomical event, such as a solstice, or by an observable change in the environment, such as the birth of new lambs or the harvest of first crops. These days, called "quarter days" and "cross quarter days" also set the times for festivals. This wheel marks the passage of the year by showing the different seasonal festivals that make up one entire cycle of seasons.

Down through the years of history, as people traveled and moved about, they took their calendars and customs with them. The earliest people to settle in North America came from northern Europe—from England, Germany, France, Spain, Scotland, and Ireland. Although, by the seventeenth and eighteenth centuries, all the people of these countries used the Roman calendar, they still celebrated certain festivals from their own particular folk heritage. These festivals came from the much older calendar that was based on seasonal changes, rather than on the mathematically fixed dates of the once powerful Roman Empire and its Church.

Revival of interest in Celtic music, dance, art, mythology, and spiritual practice

The Boston Celtics basketball team was named after the Irish ancestors of many Bostonians.

53

Why Do We Care About the Traditions of Northern Europe?

In the seventeenth century, people from different parts of northwest Europe came to North America. They came primarily from Spain, France, Germany, The Netherlands, England, Scotland, Ireland, and Wales. They left their native lands for various reasons—some were free men looking for adventure, some were slaves sent to obtain riches for their masters, some were families seeking religious freedom or better land for farming. Many of them belonged to traditional cultures.

When they arrived in North America, many continued to celebrate the holidays and tell the stories of the lands they left. As they became acquainted with this land, some changes took place. They added new elements to their stories and songs. Wherever they settled, the new land affected their traditions. More and more people from Europe arrived. As they established communities and dealt with the land across the sea and its people, they began to develop a new culture by blending parts of their old ways with newer ones. Their traditions now became a mixture of the northern European traditions

from which they came and the native traditions of North America. And of course their traditions were affected by the physical conditions in their new homeland.

These people were the ones who formed the governments of the original thirteen colonies

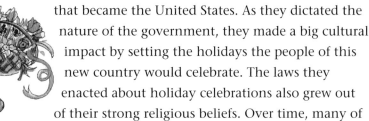

that became the United States. As they dictated the nature of the government, they made a big cultural impact by setting the holidays the people of this new country would celebrate. The laws they enacted about holiday celebrations also grew out of their strong religious beliefs. Over time, many of these religious celebrations became more secular, that is more everyday, worldly, and commercial. Elements of one holiday's celebration were combined with elements of another's, as the line between religious *holy days* and secular *holidays* became blurred. This mixture of new and old traditions slowly blended together to give us the ways we celebrate many of these same holidays today. *But because times have changed so much since earlier cultures originally celebrated these holidays, many of us no longer know where our festivals began, and how much they have altered over time.*

If we look back at the root traditions of our early settlers, we can gain a bit more understanding about our holidays now. But we need to travel back in time to sort out the various overlapping layers, to see what period in history each culture contributed to, and to learn what is at the root of each celebration.

What we learn from all of this is very simple. We see how our ancestors lived in ways that fit their time and place. And as we take the stories of the past and make them part of our lives, we allow them to grow and change with us—as we, too, must live in a way that fits our place and time, honoring the seasonal changes that repeat year after year, affecting everything that lives around us.

During the Middle Ages and Renaissance, bardic storytellers
throughout Europe retold the ancient stories of the Celts,
thus preserving the stories we still know today.

55

Glossary

barbarian: An uncivilized person. The Greeks also used the word to mean a foreigner.

bard: A tribal poet-singer skilled in compsing and reciting verses about heroes and heroines.

Beltane: A Celtic fire festival in honor of Bel, a sun god, held around the first of May.

calendar: A written method of tracking time. There are sun-based calendars, moon-based calendars, star calendars, observational calendars and many, many more.

Celt: A person who is of Celtic descent, a person of one of the Celtic tribes tied together by similarities in language and custom.

clan: A group made up of one or more families under a single leader or chief.

Coligny: An area of France where a bronze Celtic calendar was found in 1897.

divination: General name for any method of predicting the future.

Coligny calendar

Druid: A member of the priest class of the Celts. The druids were leaders politically, socially, and religiously.

Hallstadt: A place in Austria where, in 1943, a Celtic settlement from 700 B.C. was discovered.

Hallstadt Celtic decoration

equinox: The time when the sun crosses the plane of the earth's equator, making day and night of equal length.

Gaelic: The language family spoken by Celtic tribes.

Gaul: What we now know as France. Gaul was the main Celtic land in the time of Julius Caesar.

Round shield boss from England Iron Age

Imbolc: A spring festival in Gaelic-speaking countries celebrating the birth of lambs, usually held around February 1.

La Tene: A place in Switzerland where in 1850 a Celtic settlement from 500 B.C was discovered.

Lughnasa: A celebration of the first harvest, held in honor of the god Lugh, usually held around August 1.

Ogham: A type of alphabet used by the druids and later bards, based on trees, birds, animals, and so forth.

Pleiades: A cluster of stars in the constellation of Taurus, the bull, also known as the seven sisters.

Samhain: A three-day celebration that marked the end of the old year and the beginning of the new. Samhain also honored the dead. The three-day festival was held around the period between October 31 and November 2.

solstice: One of the two days when the sun is farthest from the equator.

Salt-mining tools like those excavated in La Tene

Bronze collar from England

Bibliography

Armit, Ian • *Celtic Scotland* •
London: B.T. Batsford, 1997

Carmichael, Alexander • *Carmina Gadelica* •
London: Lindisfarne Press, 1992

Costley, Sarah, and Charles Kightly • *A Celtic Book of Days* •
London: Thames and Hudson, 1998

Cunliffe, Barry • *The Celtic World* •
New York: St. Martin's Press, 1993

Dottin, Georges • *The Civilization of the Celts* •
New York: Crescent, 1970

Green, Marian • *A Calendar of Festivals* • Rockport, Mass.: Element, 1991.

Green, Miranda J. • *Dictionary of Celtic Myth and Legend* •
London: Thames and Hudson, 1992

Green, Miranda J., editor • *The Celtic World* •
London: Routledge, 1995

Laing, Lloyd and Jennifer • *Celtic Britain and Ireland* •
New York: St. Martin's Press, 1995

Markale, Jean • *The Celts* •
Rochester, Vt.: Inner Traditions, 1993

Martell, Hazel Mary • *The Celts* •
New York: Penguin Books, 1994

Matthews, Caitlín • *The Celtic Book of Days* •
Rochester, Vt; Destiny Books, 1998

———• *The Celtic Tradition* •
Rockport, Mass.: Element, 1995

Matthews, John • *Drinking from the Sacred Well* • San Francisco: HarperSanFrancisco, 1998.

Matthews, John and Caitlín • *The Winter Solstice* •
Wheaton, Ill.: Quest Books, 1998

Matthews, John, and R. J. Stewart • *Celtic Warrior Chiefs* •
London: Firebird, 1993

Pennick, Nigel • *The Pagan Book of Days* •
Rochester Vt.: Destiny Books, 1992

Powell, T. G. E. • *The Celts* •
London: Thames and Hudson, 1980

Rees, Alwyn and Brinley • *Celtic Heritage* •
London: Thames and Hudson, 1978

Ross, Anne • *Pagan Celtic Britain* •
London: Constable, 1967

——— • *Folklore of the Scottish Highlands* •
New York: Barnes and Noble, 1993

Sharkey, John • *Celtic Mysteries* •
New York: Thames and Hudson 1989

Stewart, R. J. • *Celtic Myths, Celtic Legends* •
London: Blandford, 1994

——— • *Celtic Gods, Celtic Goddesses* •
London: Blandford, 1990

Stewart, R. J., and Robin Williamson • *Celtic Bards, Celtic Druids* •
London: Blandford, 1996

Index